Butterfly counting

How many butterflies do you see?
Click on the correct number for each color.

Red butterflies
(4) (6) (7)

Blue butterflies
(3) (4) (6)

Yellow butterflies
(1) (5) (7)

Green butterflies
(3) (5) (6)

Black-and-white butterflies
(2) (3) (4)

Take quizzes about
the fun facts in this book!

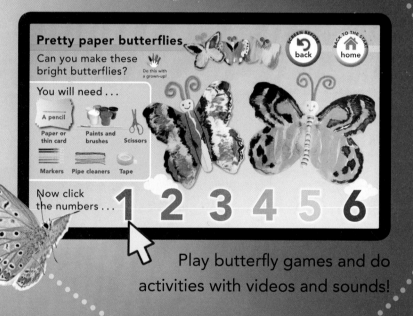

Pretty paper butterflies

Can you make these
bright butterflies?

Do this with
a grown-up!

You will need . . .

A pencil

Paper or
thin card

Paints and
brushes

Scissors

Markers   Pipe cleaners   Tape

Now click
the numbers . . . 1 2 3 4 5 6

SCREEN BEFORE
back

BACK TO THE START
home

Play butterfly games and do
activities with videos and sounds!

Log on to
www.scholastic.com/discovermore/readers
Enter this special code: **L1BBTMFN4TP1**

Come into the garden of butterflies. Look at the butterflies fly by. They are all the colors of the rainbow.

Butterflies have four wings.
They have six legs and
two antennae.

Wings

Antennae

Feeding
tube

Legs

Look at all
the shapes
and patterns!

shiny

spotted

striped

see-through

Let's watch butterflies grow and change. There are four stages in a butterfly's life.

1. Egg

2. Caterpillar

3. Chrysalis

4. Butterfly

NEW WORD

chrysalis
KRIS-uh-lis
A caterpillar changes
into a butterfly inside
a **chrysalis**.

SAY IT OUT LOUD

9

A butterfly finds a leaf
to lay its eggs on.

Egg

Some butterflies lay one egg at a time.

Others lay lots of eggs.

Butterfly eggs are different shapes and colors. They feel different, too.

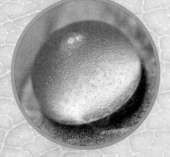

Some are smooth.

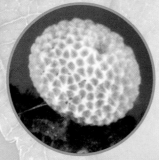

Some are bumpy.

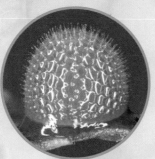

Some have spikes!

A caterpillar grows inside the egg.

It chews a hole in the shell.

It wiggles
its way out.

It eats its own shell.
Then it starts to eat
leaves. Lots of them!

Shell

The caterpillar grows and grows. Its skin gets too tight. Its tight skin splits! The caterpillar crawls out in brand-new skin. This can happen again and again.

Old skin

New skin

MARIA SIBYLLA MERIAN

Maria
lived over 300 years ago. She watched caterpillars change into butterflies. She drew amazing pictures of them.

A drawing by Maria

17

NEW WORD

shed

shed

A caterpillar **sheds** old skin four or five times.

SAY IT OUT LOUD

Soon the caterpillar stops eating. It's about to make a BIG change!

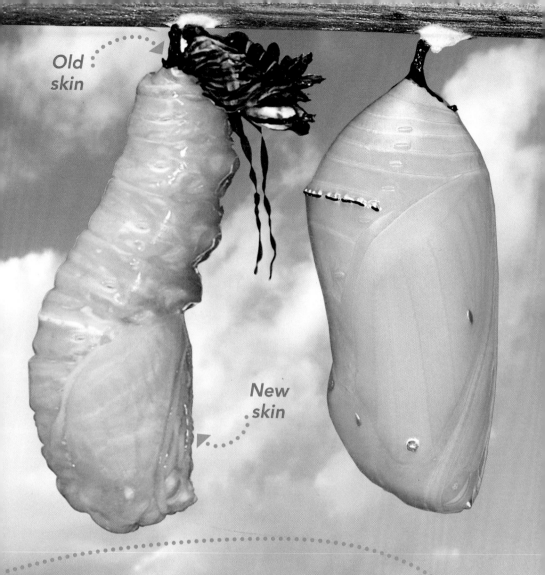

Old
skin

New
skin

It hangs head down. It
sheds its skin for the last
time. The new skin hardens
into a chrysalis.

The chrysalis
splits open!
A butterfly
pushes free.
It has soft,
wet wings.

20

Its wings are warmed by the sun. Slowly they harden and dry. The butterfly flies off for its new life with wings.

The butterfly eats sweet nectar from flowers. It can't chew. It sips through a strawlike tube.

Other butterfly food

human sweat

turtle tears

Feeding
tube

tree sap

mud puddles

rotting fruit

23

Some animals
eat butterflies.
This bird
is hungry!

24

But this butterfly
can hide. It closes
its wings. It holds
still. It looks just like
a dead leaf!

Butterflies have other ways to stay safe. Some have spots. The spots look like eyes. They scare some predators away.

Butterfly predators

lizards

frogs

26

birds

spiders

Have you seen butterflies in a garden? Plant some flowers. They may visit you!

You can have
your own garden
of butterflies.

Glossary

antenna
A feeler on the head of an insect. A butterfly has two antennae.

butterfly
An insect with a thin body and large wings. Butterflies are often colorful.

caterpillar
The second stage in a butterfly's life.

chrysalis
The hard outer shell of a butterfly that protects it as it changes from a caterpillar into an adult.

nectar
A sweet liquid from flowers.

predator
An animal that hunts and eats other animals.

sap
A liquid that carries water and food through a plant.

shed
To get rid of old outer skin so that the insect or animal inside can grow bigger.

sweat
The salty liquid that your skin makes when you are hot.

Index

A B
antennae 6

C D
caterpillar 8, 14–19
chrysalis 8, 9, 19–20
colors 4–5, 13

E
egg 8, 10–13, 14

F
feeding tube 6, 22–23
flying 21
food 15, 22–23

G
garden 28–29

H I J K
hiding 25

L
legs 6

M
Merian, Maria Sibylla 17

N O
nectar 22

P Q R
patterns 7, 26
predator 24, 26–27

S T U V
shapes 7, 13
skin 16, 18–19

W X Y Z
wings 6–7, 20–21, 25

Copyright © 2014 by Scholastic Inc.

ISBN 978-0-545-67951-0

12 11 10 9 8 7 6 5 4 3 2 1   14 15 16 17 18 19/0

Printed in the U.S.A.   40
This edition first printing, December 2014

Scholastic is constantly working to lessen the environmental
impact of our manufacturing processes. To view our
industry-leading paper procurement policy,
visit www.scholastic.com/paperpolicy.

For their generosity of time in sharing their expertise, special thanks to:
Dr. Charles Van Orden Covell, Jr., Curator of Lepidoptera, McGuire Center for
Lepidoptera and Biodiversity, Florida Museum of Natural History, University of Florida;
and Dr. Andrew Warren, Senior Collections Manager, McGuire Center for Lepidoptera
and Biodiversity, Florida Museum of Natural History, University of Florida.

Images

Alamy Images: 24 t (Ger Bosma), 17 t, 17 ct (Interfoto), 13 t inset (Survivalphotos); AP Images/Jeff Cremer/Solent News/REX: 22 br; Dreamstime: 7 br (Alessandrozocc), 2 b bg, 3 b bg (Andrey Semenov), 26 bg, 27 bg (Anhong), 2 br, 7 cfr (Bornin54), cover t bg (Bytedust), 2 tr (Colette6), 8 b inset bg, 12 bg, 13 bg (Dejan Ljami), 7 cbl (Dermot68), cover cbr (Domiciano Pablo Romero Franco), 4 b bg, 5 b bg (Elenamiv), 17 cb (Frogtravel), 1, 5 t (Gailshumway), 26 tr (Gary Uttley), 7 (Hakoar), cover main (Harald Jeske), 28 bg, 29 bg (Ivan Kmit), 18 bg, 19 bg, 20 bg, 21 bg (Jason P Ross), 10 fg, 20 t, 20 b, 21 b (Jens Stolt), 6 l (Jing Zhang), 28 fg, 29 t, 29 c (Juliasha), cover ctl (Leonidtit), cover cbl, cover tl (Lynnlauterbach), 3 cr, 4 cr (Marcouliana), 10 b bg, 11 b bg (Melinda Fawver), cover bl, cover ctr (Michal Bednarek), 26 c (Mr.smith Chetanachan), 22 bg, 23 t (Musat Christian), inside front cover cl (Naddiya), 6 bg, 7 bg, 16 t bg, 17 t bg (Nicky Jacobs), back cover (Nike Sh), 20 tl (Paul Lemke), 8 bg, 9 bg (Pimmimemom), 16 b fg, 17 b fg (Podius), cover ctc, cover tr (Rqs), 23 bc (Sever180), 18 t, 18 t branch, 19 tl, 19 t branch, 19 tr, 19 b, 20 tr, 20 t branch, 21 t branch (Stevenrussellsmithphotos), 32 main (Taiga), 26 bl (Thanarot Ngoenwilai), 4 tl (Udvarházi Irén), 10 t bg, 11 t bg (Valio84sl), 25 t (Xiaoxia Jia), 7 ctr (Yongkiet); Fotolia/Sailorr: 7 cl; iStockphoto: inside front cover tr, 32 b (Alex Belomlinsky), 5 tcr (alexomelko), 5 cbl (Antagain), 27 bl (AntonioGuillem), 4 t bg, 5 t bg, 17 b bg (bernie_moto), 16 b inset, 18 b (CathyKeifer), 22 cl, 23 cr (Ceneri), 26 br (CreativeImagery), inside front cover tl (dra_schwartz), 7 bc (Dragan2003), 8 r inset (EvaKaufman), inside front cover cr (funnybank), 24 b (GlobalP), 2 t bg, 3 t bg (GodfriedEdelman), 6 r, 7 tl, 7 cr (imv), 2 tl (johnandersonphoto), 5 tcl (kurga), 3 bl (LexiTheMonster), 23 br (Lidara), 4 tcl, 4 tc (Liliboas), 23 bl (LindaWashburnRoberts), 2 bl (Marco Marchi), 5 cbr, 7 ctc (marcouliana), inside front cover b (MarkM73), 4 tr (Myron Unrau), cursor throughout (pagadesign), 30, 31 (pailoolom), 4 b (Photo_Concepts), 27 bc (pimmimemom), 5 rainbow (plusphoto), 7 cfl (PrinPrince), 12 tl (Puleo), 29 b (RyanKing999), 22 bl (SKLA), computer monitor throughout (skodonnell), 4 cl (stanley45), 22 tl (tacojim), 5 b (thawats), 23 cr, 27 br (totallyjamie), 24 bg, 25 bg (triloks), 7 tr (Ullimi), 7 bl (varius-studios); Jacobus de Roode: 11 fg; Jay Cossey: 12 c, 13 ct inset, 13 cb inset; Mary Holland: 14 bg, 15 bg; Nature Picture Library: 27 tl (Lynn M. Stone), 27 tr (Visuals Unlimited); Science Source: 8 b inset fg (David M. Schleser/Nature's Images), 8 l inset (Nature's Images), 8 t inset (Tom Myers); Shutterstock, Inc./Henrik Larsson: 12 bl; Thinkstock/Mathisa_s: 7 ctl; Visuals Unlimited/Michael Ready: 14 t inset, 14 b inset, 15 t inset.